Social Security and Medicare for the New Millenium

Social Security and Medicare for the New Millenium

Dr. Maurice Youakim, PhD

Writers Club Press

San Jose New York Lincoln Shanghai

Social Security and Medicare for the New Millenium

Writers Club Press
an imprint of iUniverse.com, Inc.

For information address:
iUniverse.com, Inc.
620 North 48th Street, Suite 201
Lincoln, NE 68504-3467
www.iuniverse.com

ISBN: 0-595-14189-7

Printed in the United States of America

Contents

Acknowledgements

I would like to thank Mr. Robert Yammine and Mrs. Cathleen Youakim for their valuable suggestions and comments.

Introduction

The Social Security Act was signed into law on August 14, 1934. It was designed to provide a limited retirement income for workers insured under the social security system. The Social Security Act has undergone several modifications. The system has served it purpose during the last sixty five years, and is still providing economic help to millions of citizens of the United States. However, the present social security system lacks stability and resiliency for current social and economic times. Also, the current system is susceptible to fraud by those who take advantage of loop holes in the system.

A change to the existing system is a big step and requires strong leadership and foresight. Although several changes to the social security system have been made, the system did not change significantly since inception in the mid 1930s. It is the intent of the author to propose a reformed, renovated and common sense social security and medicare system that will satisfy the future needs of the majority of United States citizens.

The author will present the subject matter in simple terms and give examples where necessary. The book will describe a realistic and a practical plan which will provide for all residents a good and lasting source of income during their retirement years. Most importantly, the proposed plan can be accomplished without overtaxing individuals. This book will discuss in detail the method by which social security and medicare should be managed in the 21st century and beyond.

Chapter 1

Overview of the Current System

The Social Security Act was signed into law on August 14, 1934. It was designed to provide a limited retirement income for workers insured under the social security system. In this chapter we discuss briefly the current social security and medicare rules and benefits and present an example to illustrate how the current system works. The following rules and benefits are extracted from the social security administration pamphlets and web site at http://www.ssa.gov. In some instances the wording is modified to clarify the intent of the rules.

Earning Record:

The Social Security Administration keeps a lifetime record of earnings reported under an individual's name and social security number. When the individual applies for social security benefits, the Social Security Administration checks the individual's earning record to see if he or she worked long enough to qualify, and then use their earnings to determine the amount of the monthly benefits.

Maximum Earnings:

The maximum amount of yearly earnings taxed by social security is set by law. The individual and the individual's employer pay social security taxes on earnings up to this maximum limit. The 2000 maximum earnings limit is $76,200.00.

Tax Rate:

In the year 2000 the tax rate for each, the individual and individual's employer, was 6.20% for social security and 1.45% for medicare. A total tax on earnings for each employed individual is 15.30%. Social security tax applies up to the Maximum Earnings limit, while medicare tax applies to all earnings with no upper limit on earnings.

Social Security Credits:

To qualify for benefits, an individual needs to earn "credits" through work. In the year 2000, an individual could earn one credit for each $780.00 of wages or self-employment earned. When an individual earned $3120.00, the individual earned the yearly maximum of 4 credits. Most individuals need 40 credits (10 years of work) earned over their working lifetime to receive retirement benefits. For disability and survivor's benefits, younger individuals need fewer credits to be eligible.

Social Security Benefits:

Social security benefits are based on an individual's earnings over their working career, up to the Maximum Earnings Limit (not on the taxes paid). To figure an individual's benefit, the Social Security Administration updates the individual's earnings to take account of changes in the national average wage from the time the individual started to work until the individual reaches the age of 60, becomes disabled or dies. These adjusted earnings are averaged together and a formula is applied to the average to arrive at a benefit amount. This amount may be reduced at the time the individual applies if the individual received workers' compensation, a public disability benefit or a pension based on work not covered by social security. The amount the spouse receives may also be reduced if the spouse receives a government pension.

The social security retirement benefits will replace only part of the individual's pre-retirement earnings. The replacement rate ranges from about 60 per cent of pre-retirement earnings for a worker who has always earned the minimum wage to about 26 per cent for a worker who has always earned the maximum covered by social security. *In the year 2000, the average monthly social security benefit paid to a retired worker at age 65 or older is $1373.00. The maximum monthly social security benefit paid to a retired worker at age 65 or older is $1433.00.*

Retirement Benefits:

An individual can get reduced benefits as early as age 62 or get full retirement at age 65. Starting in the year 2000 for individuals born in 1938 or later, this age will increase gradually. By the year 2027, full retirement age will be 67 for individuals born after 1959.

Disability benefits:

These benefits are paid if an individual becomes totally disabled before reaching full retirement age. To get disability benefits, an individual must meet these three conditions:

a. The individual must have a certain number of credits earned during a specific period of time.

b. The individual must have a physical or mental condition that has lasted or is expected to last at least 12 months or end only after the individual's death.

c. The individual's disability must be severe enough to prevent the citizen from doing any substantial work, including the last job.

Benefits for the family:

As the individual works, she or he builds up protection for their family. Benefits may be payable to:

a. Any unmarried children under age 18 (under age 19 if in high school) or 18 and older if child is disabled before the age of 22.

b. Individual's spouse who is age 62 or older or who is any age and caring for the individual's qualified child who is under age 16 or disabled.

c. Individual's divorced spouse who was married to individual for at least 10 years and who is age 62 or older and unmarried.

Unmarried young or disabled children may qualify for monthly payments. An individual's widow/widower even if divorced may also qualify for payments starting:

a. At age 60 or at age 50 if disabled (if divorced, individual's marriage must have lasted at least 10 years).

b. At any age if caring for individual's qualified child who is under age 16 or disabled child.

An individual's spouse cannot get both her or his benefits plus benefits from individual's record. Only the amount equal to the larger of the two benefits will be paid.

Usually each family member qualifies for a monthly benefit that is up to 50 per cent of the individual's retirement or a disability benefit subject to a limit. The limit on the amount paid depends on the amount of the individual's benefits and the number of family members who also qualify. The total varies, but is generally equal to about 150 to 180 per cent of individual's retirement benefits (it may be less for disability benefits). This limit also applies to benefits paid to survivors.

Medicare benefits:

Medicare hospital and medical insurance is a two-part benefit program that helps protect individuals from the high costs of medical care. Hospital insurance benefits (Part A) help pay the cost when an individual is in the hospital and for certain kinds of follow-up care. Medical insurance benefits (Part B) help pay the costs of doctor services.

If an individual has enough work credits, she or he may qualify for Medicare hospital insurance at age 65, even if an individual is still working. An individual may qualify before age 65 if disabled or have permanent kidney failure. The individual's spouse may also qualify for hospital insurance at age 65 because of the individual's working record.

Almost anyone who is 65 or older or who qualifies for Medicare hospital insurance can enroll for medical insurance. An individual must pay a monthly premium for it.

For more detailed information on existing social security and medicare programs, call or write to the Social Security Administration office closest to you.

An Example of a Retiree Under The Present System

Currently, an employee who is gainfully employed is taxed on her or his gross income. The taxes include federal, state, social security and medicare. Let us say that the social security and medicare tax is about 7.65% of the employee's income. The employer contributes another 7.65% to the employee's social security and medicare taxes. Together, the employee and the employer are paying 15.3% social security and medicare taxes. The social security tax has a yearly upper limit of gross earnings while the medicare tax has no upper limit. The yearly upper limit of social security tax on gross income increases yearly

As an example, assume that Cindy works for XYZ Inc. and earns $50,000.00 a year in salary. The current 7.65% tax is divided between social security and Medicare tax as 6.2% and 1.45% respectively. Our employee Cindy will pay $3100.00, and her employer XYZ Inc. will pay $3100.00 in social security tax. Also, Cindy will pay $725.00, and her employer will pay $725.00 in medicare tax. In effect, in one year the government received $6,200.00 in social security tax and $1,450.00 in medicare tax on behalf of the employee, Cindy. If we assume that the employee, Cindy, works for 30 years for XYZ Inc., and her salary stayed the same for all this period, then the employee, Cindy, and her company would have paid $186,000.00 in social security tax and $43,500.00 in medicare tax.

Let us say that our example employee, Cindy, retires in the year 2001 at age 62 with a life expectancy of 28 years. That is, we are assuming that the employee, Cindy will live to a ripe age of 90 and will collect social security until age 90 (national life expectancy for women is 80 years, in this book life expectancy will be the national life expectancy of 80 plus 10 years). The current system will pay our employee, Cindy, the sum of about $1,015.00 a month, a total of $12,180.00 per year and $341,040.00 for a lifetime.

Chapter 2

Overview of the Proposed System

Every person born in the United States Of America (USA) is issued a social security number. If a person immigrates to the USA, he or she is issued a social security number. Any foreign national residing in the USA who becomes a legal immigrant of the USA is issued a social security number. Therefore, we shall assume that the social security number is a unique identifier of each legal resident of the USA. Using her or his social security number, every individual in the USA should have two bank accounts in a bank we shall call the Social Security and Medicare Bank. One account is for their monthly social security payments during their retirement years and the other account is for their medical care during retirement years. The capital city of each state of the USA will house one Social Security and Medicare Bank. The 50 Social Security and Medicare Banks will be administered by the Social Security Administration and the employees will be paid from a fraction of the interest accrued on the accounts deposited in the Social Security and Medicare Banks. The current social security rules and regulations will have to be modified to keep up with the times. The rules must lend themselves to the 21st century and beyond.

As each individual is working, her or his account balances in one of the Social Security and Medicare Banks grow. The 50 Social Security and Medicare Banks invest that money in a guaranteed plan and manage the distribution of the money during the retirement years.

If the individual is younger than 62 years and passes away, the balance of the individual's account is credited to their spouse's account if married, and the individual's account is closed. Otherwise, if the individual is not married and has no dependent children, the balance of the individual account is transferred to the GENERAL account and the individual account is closed.

When an individual reaches the age of 62, she or he applies to receive the distribution from her or his individual account. The individual will receive a monthly distribution from her or his account based on the total amount in her or his account and on her or his life expectancy. The simple distribution formula described in chapter 6 will be used to disburse the payments to the retirees. Upon the individual's death, if the individual is married, his or her account balance will be transferred to their wife's or husband's account balance, and the deceased individual's account will be closed. If the deceased individual does not have a wife or a husband or dependent children, the balance of the individual's account will be credited to the GENERAL account in the Social Security and Medicare Bank and the deceased individual's account will be closed.

The present social security and medicare qualifications rules apply to the proposed plan. That is, any individual who reaches the age of 62 and did not pay into her or his own social security and medicare accounts, should use her or his own life savings to live on, apply to the welfare department for assistance, or work. The Social Security and Medicare Banks are not a handout system. It is a system for individuals who worked for many years and saved for her or his future

Remember Cindy in chapter 1; Under our proposed plan, if the government would invest Cindy's social security tax of $6,200.00 yearly in a certificate of deposit earning a maximum of 7% per year, after 30 years our employee would have as capital more than $600,000.00 (at 6% per year, it will be more than $519,000.00).

Then, at age 62, our employee, Cindy could withdraw the yearly interest on her capital. ***The interest on $600,000.00 is at least $30,000.00 at the rate of 5% only! And still our employee, Cindy, would have her $600,000.00 as capital.***

In the following chapters we present details of the proposed Social Security and Medicare Banks, investment of funds, salaries and benefits to bank employees, deposits and withdrawals to individual accounts, and individual's health insurance (Medicare).

Chapter 3

Social Security and Medicare Banks

In every state of the USA there will be a Social Security and Medicare Bank located in the capital city. There will be a total of 50 Social Security and Medicare Banks.

The management and regulations of the Social Security and Medicare Banks will be under the jurisdiction of the Social Security and Medicare Administration. This administration should be capable of managing the Social Security and Medicare Banking System operations including management, investments and disbursements.

The Social Security and Medicare Banking System consists of all the Social Security and Medicare Banks located in the capital city of every state of the USA. The 50 Social Security and Medicare Bank branches should be connected by a computer network to allow the transfer of funds from one of these banks to another. An individual working in more than one state should specify where should her or his Social Security and Medicare account be located.

Only one bank within the banking system is permitted to carry their Social Security and Medicare accounts. Assume an individual is working in Illinois and her or his accounts are in Springfield, Illinois. If this individual is moving to California, then the individual should write a letter requesting a transfer of her or his accounts to the Social Security and Medicare Bank in Sacramento, California.

The Social Security and Medicare Banking System will be headed by the Vice President of the United States. The director of each Social Security and Medicare Bank could be nominated by the governor of the state where the branch is located and confirmed by the state senate or the process will follow the one used for directors of the Federal Reserve Banking System. Each director's term should be limited to a maximum of four years and should coincide with the presidential election year.

To start with, the current social security employees will be the Social Security and Medicare Banking System employees. Their salaries and benefits will be derived from investments of the accounts deposited in the Social Security and Medicare Banks. For example, if the accounts are generating 6% interest, then 1% of the 6% might be used to defray the cost of payroll, benefits and overhead expenses of the banking system.

The current rate of social security and medicare tax is 15.3%. The current social security and medicare tax has built-in increases in the tax rate and the maximum earnings amount the employees are taxed on. Currently, the federal government and many elected politicians refer to the surplus of tax money in the coming years. What do they mean by surplus? Since the tax rate keeps increasing and the maximum earnings amount individuals being taxed on is also increasing, the tax money collected by the federal government each year will be more than they budgeted for, and that is what they call surplus. In effect, we the residents of the USA are overtaxed to support the Washington bureaucracy. Whenever government officials feel that they are in a position of power and they have excess money in their budgets, they tend to create a new venture or department to spend the excess money. Otherwise their budgets for the coming fiscal year will be cut by the budget committee. Remember the phrase "USE IT OR LOSE IT"; that is the government officials' motto and we don't like it.

In our proposed plan, future tax rates on Social Security and medicare will remain constant and might even decrease. For simplicity, we shall assume a fixed tax rate of 16% for the next 30 years. With this tax rate, we plan to phase out the current system over the 30-year period by allocating percentages to the currently retired population and the working population. Our plan divides the population into 3 categories: individuals under 30 years of age are in category 1, the individuals between 30 and 62 years of age are in category 2, and individuals above 62 years of age are in category 3.

As an example, let us take a look at the following three tables, where the percent allocations have been calculated for working individuals earning $20,000.00 per year in table 1, $50,000.00 per year in table 2 or $80,000.00 per year in table 3. These three tables apply to individuals 30-62 years of age, that is, those in category 2. The percent allocation shown in the tables is the amount of money that will be deposited in their accounts within the Social Security and Medicare Banking System. The difference between the amount shown and 16% of their earnings will be deposited in a GENERAL Social Security and Medicare account within the same banking system. The GENERAL account will be used to continue the current social security systems payouts. Also, it will be used to pay retirees during the 30-year transition period and beyond until the current system is totally phased out. Any surplus in the GENERAL account will stay in the Social Security and Medicare Banking System to augment the income of the residents who were between the ages of 30 and 62 when the transition started and to lower the social security and medicare tax rate in the future.

In tables 1, 2 and 3 the first column contains the transition years starting with year 2001, the second column contains the percentage that will be allocated to the working individual's account during the transition years, the third column contains the amount deposited in the working individual's account based on the second column percentage, and the fourth column contains the amount deposited in the GENERAL account using the difference between 16% social security tax rate and the percentage allocated to the working individual's account shown in the second column.

Table 1. Per cent allocation for individuals 30-62 years of age earning $20,000.00 per year.

Year	Individual account Percent	Individual account	GENERAL account Percent	GENERAL account
2001	1%	$200	15%	$3000
2002	1%	$200	15%	$3000
2003	2%	$400	14%	$2800
2004	2%	$400	14%	$2800
2005	3%	$600	13%	$2600
2006	3%	$600	13%	$2600
2007	4%	$800	12%	$2400
2008	4%	$800	12%	$2400
2009	5%	$1000	11%	$2200
2010	5%	$1000	11%	$2200
2011	6%	$1200	10%	$2000

2012	6%	$1200	10%	$2000
2013	7%	$1400	9%	$1800
2014	7%	$1400	9%	$1800
2015	8%	$1600	8%	$1600
2016	8%	$1600	8%	$1600
2017	9%	$1800	7%	$1400
2018	9%	$1800	7%	$1400
2019	10%	$2000	6%	$1200
2020	10%	$2000	6%	$1200
2021	11%	$2200	5%	$1000
2022	11%	$2200	5%	$1000
2023	12%	$2400	4%	$800
2024	12%	$2400	4%	$800
2025	13%	$2600	3%	$600
2026	13%	$2600	3%	$600

2027	14%	$2800	2%	$400
2028	14%	$2800	2%	$400
2029	15%	$3000	1%	$200
2030	15%	$3000	1%	$200
2031	16%	$3200	0%	$0

Table 2. Per cent allocation for individuals 30-62 years of age earning $50,000.00 per year.

Year	Individual account Percent	Individual account	GENERAL account Percent	GENERAL account
2001	1%	$500	15%	$7500
2002	1%	$500	15%	$7500
2003	2%	$1000	14%	$7000
2004	2%	$1000	14%	$7000
2005	3%	$1500	13%	$6500

2006	3%	$1500	13%	$6500
2007	4%	$2000	12%	$6000
2008	4%	$2000	12%	$6000
2009	5%	$2500	11%	$5500
2010	5%	$2500	11%	$5500
2011	6%	$3000	10%	$5000
2012	6%	$3000	10%	$5000
2013	7%	$3500	9%	$4500
2014	7%	$3500	9%	$4500
2015	8%	$4000	8%	$4000
2016	8%	$4000	8%	$4000
2017	9%	$4500	7%	$3500

2018	9%	$4500	7%	$3500
2019	10%	$5000	6%	$3000
2020	10%	$5000	6%	$3000
2021	11%	$5500	5%	$2500
2022	11%	$5500	5%	$2500
2023	12%	$6000	4%	$2000
2024	12%	$6000	4%	$2000
2025	13%	$6500	3%	$1500
2026	13%	$6500	3%	$1500
2027	14%	$7000	2%	$1000
2028	14%	$7000	2%	$1000
2029	15%	$7500	1%	$500
2030	15%	$7500	1%	$500
2031	16%	$8000	0%	$0

Table 3. Per cent allocation for individuals 30-62 years of age earning $80,000.00 per year.

Year	Individual account Percent	Individual account	GENERAL account Percent	GENERAL account
2001	1%	$800	15%	$12000
2002	1%	$800	15%	$12000
2003	2%	$1600	14%	$11200
2004	2%	$1600	14%	$11200
2005	3%	$2400	13%	$10400
2006	3%	$2400	13%	$10400
2007	4%	$3200	12%	$9600
2008	4%	$3200	12%	$9600
2009	5%	$4000	11%	$8800
2010	5%	$4000	11%	$8800
2011	6%	$4800	10%	$8000

2012	6%	$4800	10%	$8000
2013	7%	$5600	9%	$7200
2014	7%	$5600	9%	$7200
2015	8%	$6400	8%	$6400
2016	8%	$6400	8%	$6400
2017	9%	$7200	7%	$5600
2018	9%	$7200	7%	$5600
2019	10%	$8000	6%	$4800
2020	10%	$8000	6%	$4800
2021	11%	$8800	5%	$4000
2022	11%	$8800	5%	$4000
2023	12%	$9600	4%	$3200
2024	12%	$9600	4%	$3200
2025	13%	$10400	3%	$2400

2026	13%	$10400	3%	$2400
2027	14%	$11200	2%	$1600
2028	14%	$11200	2%	$1600
2029	15%	$12000	1%	$800
2030	15%	$12000	1%	$800
2031	16%	$12800	0%	$0

In the proposed Social Security and Medicare Banking System all employees will receive their salaries and benefits from proceeds of the investments. The investments will be limited to

a) Treasury Bills
b) US federal and state agencies
c) Municipal bonds
d) AAA rated companies
e) Guaranteed real estate investments
f) Financial institutions

to name a few. A team of investment experts including the federal reserve directors will be some of the new Social Security and Medicare Banking System advisors that will wisely invest the huge amount of capital that the system will have on hand. Investments must be discussed at length by the above experts to arrive at a plan of investment that will guarantee the capital as well as the return on investment.

In our proposed plan, residents of each state will have their Social Security and Medicare accounts automatically opened in the Social Security and Medicare Banks in their state. During their employment years, their contributions plus the contribution from their employer, a total of 16% of their income, will be deposited in their account either monthly or quarterly (employer contribution should be after tax so that retirees do not have to pay taxes on their social security income).

Category 1 deposits:

For individuals who are under age 30 years at the time of implementation of the new system, the total amount contributed by the individuals and their employer will be credited to their account.

Category 2 deposits:

For individuals between the ages of 30 and 62 at the time of implementation of the new system, the amount credited to his or her account and to the GENERAL account will follow the percentage allocation for each year during the transition period as depicted in Tables 1, 2 or 3.

Category 3 deposits:

For individuals who are 62 years or older at the time of implementation of the new system, the total amount contributed by individuals and employers will be credited to the GENERAL account.

Chapter 4

Further Explanation of the Proposed Social Security and Medicare Banking System

In chapter 3, tables 1, 2 and 3 are just one example of how social security tax collected from the general public is allocated to each individual's account and to the GENERAL account. Tables 1, 2 and 3 apply to individuals in category 2 who are between the ages of 30 and 62 years of age. For individuals who are younger than 30 years of age, all the social security and medicare tax collected on their behalf will be deposited in their accounts at the Social Security and Medicare Bank. For individuals who are 62 years and older, the present social security plan will be used. The following discussion will elaborate on these 3 categories.

Income of $20K:

A. Category 1(individual's age under 30 years):

As noted earlier, this group does not follow table 1 allocations; instead all their social security and medicare tax goes directly into their account. They have at least 32 years to build their social security and medicare accounts. These individuals will have $3200.00 deposited yearly in their accounts. None of the 16% goes into the GENERAL account. If we assume their accounts yield 6% interest yearly, then the total value of each of their accounts after 30 years will be approximately $268,000.00. If the individual is 62 years old when she or he retires, then at the rate of 6% interest, this individual will receive $16,080.00 yearly in interest income without touching the principal of $268,000.00. As we will see later, the individual could receive an extra yearly amount if we assume that the individual's account will be depleted within the computed individual's life expectancy.

B. Category 2(individual's age between 30 and 62 years):

In this category, individuals have 32 or fewer years to build their social security and medicare accounts. Individuals in this category follow the per cent allocation of table 1 (see in chapter 3), i.e. part of their social security tax is deposited in their account and the remaining part of the 16% tax is deposited in the GENERAL account. At the time of retirement, each individual in this category will be treated on a case-by-case basis. Individuals with ages closer to the 30 years old cut-off age will have larger sums of money in their accounts than those closer to 62 years old. However, each of these individuals will receive **at least** the same income they would have received under the existing Social Security and Medicare System. Therefore, when applying the formula for withdrawal (see chapter 6), individuals with low balance accounts will have a choice, either to receive distribution from their account or to receive payments based on the existing social security system depending on which dollar amount is greater. If they elected to receive payments based on the existing social security system, the additional funds they will receive will be coming from the GENERAL account of the proposed Social Security and Medicare Banking System.

C. Category 3(individual's age 62 years and older):

In this category, individuals will be treated under the rules and regulations of the existing social security system. That is, their current payment will come from the GEN-ERAL account of this proposed Social Security and Medicare Bank System.

Income of $50K:

A. Category 1(individual's age under 30 years):

As noted earlier, this group does not follow table 2 allocations and all their social security and Medicare tax goes directly into their account. They have at least 32 years to build their social security and medicare accounts. These individuals will have $8,000.00 yearly deposited in their respective accounts and none of the 16% goes into the GENERAL account. If we assume their accounts yield 6% interest yearly, then the total value of each of their accounts after 30 years will be approximately $670,400.00. If the individual is 62 years old when she or he retires, then at the rate of 6% interest, this individual will receive $40,224.00 yearly in interest income, without touching the principal. As we will see later, the individual could receive an extra yearly amount if we assume that the individual's account will be depleted within the computed individual's life expectancy.

B. Category 2(individual's age between 30 and 62 years):

In this category, individuals have 32 or fewer years to build their social security and medicare accounts. Individuals in this category follow the per cent allocation of table 2 (see chapter 3), i.e. part of their social security tax is deposited in their account and the remaining part of the 16% tax is deposited in the GENERAL account. At the time of retirement, each individual in this category will be treated on a case-by-case basis. Individuals with ages closer to the 30 years old cut-off age have larger sums of money in their accounts than those closer to 62 years old. However, each of these individuals will receive **at least** the same income they would have received under the existing Social Security and Medicare System. Therefore, when applying the formula for withdrawal (see chapter 6), individuals with low balance accounts will have a choice, either to receive distribution from their account or to receive payments based on the present social security system, whichever dollar amount is greater. If they elected to receive payments based on the existing social security system, the additional funds they will receive will be coming from the GENERAL account of the proposed Social Security and Medicare Bank System.

C. Category 3(individual's age 62 years and older):

In this category, individuals will be treated under the rules and regulations of the existing social security system. That is, their current payment will come from the GENERAL account of this proposed Social Security and Medicare Bank System.

Income of $80K:

A. Category 1(individual's age under 30 years):

As noted earlier, this group does not follow table 3 allocations and all their social security and medicare tax goes directly into their account. They have at least 32 years to build their social security and medicare accounts. These individuals will have $12,800.00 yearly deposited in their respective accounts and none of the 16% goes into the GENERAL account. If we assume their accounts yield 6% interest yearly, then the total value of each of their accounts after 30 years will be approximately $1,072,640.00. If the individual is 62 years old when she or he retires, then at the rate of 6% interest, this individual will receive $64,358.00 yearly in interest income without touching the principal. As we see later, the individual could receive an extra yearly amount if we assume that the individual's account will be depleted within the computed individual's life expectancy.

B. Category 2(individual's age between 30 and 62 years):

In this category, individuals have 32 or fewer years to build their social security and medicare accounts. Individuals in this category follow the per cent allocation of table 3 (see chapter 3), i.e. part of their social security tax is deposited in their account and the remaining part of the 16% tax is deposited in the GENERAL account. At the time of retirement, each individual in this category will be treated on a case-by-case basis. Individuals with ages closer to the 30 years old cut-off age have larger sums of money in their accounts than those closer to 62 years old. However, each of these individuals will receive **at least** the same income they would have received under the existing social security and medicare system. Therefore, when applying the formula for withdrawal (see chapter 6), individuals with low balance accounts will have a choice, either to receive distribution from their account or to receive payments based on the present social security system, whichever dollar amount is greater. If they elected to receive payments based on the existing social security system, the additional funds they will receive will be coming from the GENERAL account of the proposed Social Security and Medicare Bank System.

C. Category 3(individual's age 62 years and older):

In this category, individuals will be treated under the rules and regulations of the existing social security system. That is, their current payment will come from the GENERAL account of this proposed Social Security and Medicare Bank System.

Chapter 5

Potential Tax Income and Distribution

If we assume that 100 million of the USA population is gainfully employed and the average income of an individual from the working population is about $30,000.00, then in the first year alone, funds in the GENERAL account of the proposed Social Security and Medicare Banking System will exceed 480 billion dollars. Let us assume that we have about 30 million retirees the first year during the transition period, and each of these retirees collects on the average $12,000.00 a year. The total amount that the retirees will use during the first year is approximately 360 billion dollars allowing approximately 120 billion dollars surplus in the GENERAL account. In the second year another 480 billion dollars will be collected from the working population and put in the GENERAL Social Security and Medicare account for payment to the retirees during the second year of the transition period. With the assumption of 100 million employees and 30 millions retirees, the GENERAL account in the Social Security and Medicare banks will have over 240 billion dollars for the first two years of transition. This amount does not include any interest accrued on the GENERAL account during the two transitional years, that is year 2001 and year 2002. Our 240 billion dollars **surplus** is real money and not the **potential surplus** that present elected officials and politicians speak-of in their campaigns, scaring and/or confusing the public. The GENERAL account in our Social Security and Medicare Banking System model contains a real and current balance of dollars.

At the beginning of this chapter we presented the example of 2 years income from Social Security and Medicare tax and the example of 2 years distribution based on the assumed number of gainfully employed individuals and number of expected retirees. In the following sections, we present 2 tables to demonstrate the viability and solvency of our proposed Social Security and Medicare Banking System. Table 4 shows the potential income from Social Security and Medicare tax assuming the average income of an individual in the USA is $30,000.00, $35,000.00, or $40,000.00 versus the number of gainfully employed as 100, 105, 110, 115, 120, 125, or 130 million individuals. Table 5 depicts the average social security payments of $10,000.00, $12,000.00, or $14,000.00 yearly versus the number of retirees of 30, 33, 36, 39, 42, 45, or 48 million.

Table 4. Annual Social Security and Medicare tax @ 16% Collected for the GENERAL Account.

Employees	$30K income	$35K income th	$40K income
100 million	$480 billion	$560 billion	$640 billion
105 million	$504 billion	$588 billion	$672 billion
110 million	$528 billion	$616 billion	$704 billion
115 million	$552 billion	$644 billion	$736 billion
120 million	$576 billion	$672 billion	$768 billion
125 million	$600 billion	$700 billion	$800 billion

Table 5. Payments from the GENERAL Account to Retirees.

Retirees	$10K social security payment	$12K social security payment	$14K social security payment
30 million	$300 billion	$360 billion	$420 billion
33 million	$330 billion	$396 billion	$462 billion
36 million	$360 billion	$432 billion	$504 billion
39 million	$390 billion	$468 billion	$546 billion
42 million	$420 billion	$504 billion	$588 billion
45 million	$450 billion	$540 billion	$630 billion

According to the government census of 1990, the number of individuals gainfully employed is about 110 million and the average wage earner receives about $35,000.00 in salary.

Looking at table 4, one finds that the potential income to Social Security and Medicare tax bank accounts to be 616 billion dollars. Also, according to the same sources, the average yearly payment to each retiree is about $10,800.00 and the number of retirees is about 33 million. If we look in table 5 we find that the amount paid out is approximately 396 billion dollars. Subtracting expenditure from income, 616-396=220 billion dollars in surplus. Let us assume that 20 billion dollars is overhead expenses such as employee salaries and benefits, buildings, etc. We are left with **200 billion dollars in surplus** in the GENERAL account. This is only in the first year. This type of surplus will continue to accumulate during the transition period of 30 years. In our proposed plan, the surplus in the GENERAL account will be used to increase the income of the retirees.

Chapter 6

Formula for Distribution at Retirement age of 62 years or Older

Based on a complicated formula, the current Social Security Administration issues checks for each individual that paid into the social security system. The monthly amount paid out is based upon the individual's total contribution to the social security system. The current system requires an individual to work 40 quarters before she or he is eligible to receive social security at retirement. There is a minimum amount that the administration pays out to individuals who contributed less than the minimum required contribution. In some cases, the current administration pays out to individuals who never contributed to the social security system. We would like to emphasize that the welfare system and not the social security system, should take care of individuals who did not contribute to the social security system or those who contributed less than 40 quarters.

In the following discussion, we derive a formula that will determine the amount a retiree will receive at the age of 62 years or older. Following the derivation we will apply the formula to a number of cases and discuss the results. These cases include single individuals, married individuals, divorced individuals, widowed individuals, children of deceased individuals, and disabled individuals. The formula for withdrawals during retirement years at age 62 years or older is as follows:

Let i be the interest, P be the principal in the account, W be the annual withdrawal amount, then assume yearly compounding we have the following equations:

Year 1:
$$P_1 = (P_0 - W)(1+i)$$
Year 2:
$$P_2 = (P_1 - W)(1+i)$$
$$= (P_0 - W)(1+i)(1+i) - W(1+i)$$

•

•

Year n:
$$P_n = P_0(1+i)^n - W[(1+i)^n + (1+i)^{n-1} + \ldots + (1+i)^1]$$
$$= P_0(1+i)^n - W\Sigma(1+i)^n$$

If we assume that the individual's account in the social security bank will be depleted, i.e. the balance will be zero, then our formula for the yearly withdrawal will be:

$$W = P_0(1+i)^n / \Sigma(1+i)^n$$

Now suppose that we would like to invest the same amount P_0, for a period of n years, at the fixed rate of i percent. The final value of our investment Pn , would follow the following formula:

Year 1:
$$\mathbf{P_1 = P_0\,(1+i)}$$
Year 2:
$$\mathbf{P_2 = P_1(1+i) + P_0(1+i)}$$
$$\mathbf{= P_0(1+i)(1+i) + P_0(1+i) = P_0\,[(1+i)^2 + (1+i)]}$$

•

•

Year n:
$$\mathbf{P_n = P_0[\Sigma(1+i)^n]}$$

The 6% and 7% interest rate **i**, the power factors $(1+i)^n$, and the summation factor $\Sigma(1+i)^n$, over a 30 year period is shown in table 6. The above formulas are used in the examples given in the next chapters.

Table 6. 6% and 7% interest factors used in formula of chapter 6 over a 30 year period.

n	$(1+.06)^n$	$\Sigma(1+.06)^n$	$(1+.07)^n$	$\Sigma(1+.07)^n$
1	1.06	1.06	1.07	1.07
2	1.1236	2.1836	1.1449	2.2149
3	1.1910	3.3746	1.2250	3.4399
4	1.2624	4.6370	1.3107	4.7506
5	1.3382	5.9752	1.4025	6.1531
6	1.4185	7.3937	1.5007	7.6538
7	1.5036	8.8973	1.6057	9.2595
8	1.5938	10.4911	1.7181	10.9776
9	1.6894	12.1805	1.8384	12.8160
10	1.7908	13.9713	1.9671	14.7831
11	1.8982	15.8695	2.1048	16.8879
12	2.0121	17.8816	2.2521	19.1400
13	2.1329	20.0145	2.4098	21.5498
14	2.2609	22.2754	2.5785	24.1283
15	2.3965	24.6719	2.7590	26.8873

16	2.5403	27.2122	2.9521	29.8394
17	2.6927	29.9049	3.1588	32.9982
18	2.8543	32.7592	3.3799	36.3781
19	3.0255	35.7847	3.6165	39.9946
20	3.2071	38.9918	3.8696	43.8642
21	3.3995	42.3913	4.1405	48.0047
22	3.6035	45.9948	4.4304	52.4351
23	3.8197	49.8145	4.7405	57.1756
24	4.0489	53.8634	5.0724	62.2480
25	4.2918	58.1552	5.4274	67.6754
26	4.5493	62.7045	5.8073	73.4827
27	4.8223	67.5268	6.2138	79.6965
28	5.1116	72.6384	6.6488	86.3453
29	5.4183	78.0567	7.1142	93.4595
30	5.7434	83.8001	7.6122	101.0717

Chapter 7

Social Security Payments to Single Individuals

A single individual, who satisfied the 40 quarters requirement, has his or her own social security account in the bank of the proposed social security system. His or her account should be credited with **at least 40 quarters** before the individual becomes eligible for any distribution. Assuming that this individual meets the criteria just described, then this individual will receive a yearly income from his or her account based on the formula derived in chapter 6. The life expectancy number of years after retirement, n, in the formula will be dictated by the national average of life expectancy plus 10 years. For example, if life expectancy for men is 76 and for women it is 80, then n in the formula will be n=(86–retirement age) years for men and n=(90–retirement age) years for women.

Current retirees, i.e. retirees under the existing social security system, who are 62 years or older are not affected by this distribution.

Example 1: category 1(under 30 years of age)

In category 1, individuals are expected to work and contribute to their social security and medicare accounts during their 30 to 40 years of potential employment. If their average annual income is $20000.00, then at 6% per year return rate, their social security and medicare account will be at least $268,000.00 after 30 years.

However, for example 1, let us assume that the individual is a single man who did not contribute that much to his social security and medicare accounts during his 30 or 40 years of potential employment. Let us assume that his account balance in the Social Security and Medicare Bank is only $56,000.00 instead of $268,000.00. If this individual retired at age 62, then his life expectancy, n, after retirement will be n=86-62=24 years. If we assume 6% return on investing his account balance and that his account balance will be depleted (i.e. zero) within 24 years, then according to the formula of chapter 6, the annual payments to the individual will be about $4,210.00. On the other hand, if we assume 6% return on investing his account balance, keeping his account balance of $56,000.00 after 24 years, then the annual payments to the individual will be about $3,360.00. The difference between annual payments of $4,210.00, depleting his account balance within 24 years, and annual payments of $3,360.00, keeping his account balance after 24 years, is $850.00. Our individual could receive $3,360.00+½($850.00)=$3,785.00 annually. The ½ factor extends the individual's account balance beyond

30 years instead of depleting the account balance within 24 years. Once the account balance is depleted (i.e. zero), the annual payments of $3,785.00 will come from the GENERAL account if the individual is still living. If the yearly distribution of $3,785.00 is below the expected living standards set by the government, then our single man should apply to the welfare department for additional money.

Example 2: category 1 (under 30 years of age)

In category 1, individuals are expected to work and contribute to their social security and medicare accounts during their 30 to 40 years of potential employment. If their average annual income is $20,000.00, then at 6% per year return rate, their social security and medicare account will be at least $268,000.00 after 30 years.

However, for example 2, let us assume that the individual is a single woman who did not contribute that much to her social security and medicare accounts during her 30 or 40 years of potential employment. Let us assume that her account balance in the Social Security and Medicare Bank is only $56,000.00 instead of $268,000.00. If this individual retired at age 62, then her life expectancy, n, after retirement will be n=90-62=28 years. If we assume 6% return on investing her account balance and that her account balance will be depleted (i.e. zero) within 28 years, then according to the formula of chapter 6, the annual payments to the individual will be about $3,940.00. On the other hand, if we assume 6%

return on investing her account balance keeping her account balance of $56,000.00 after 28 years, then the annual payments to the individual will be about $3,360.00. The difference between annual payments of $3,940.00, depleting her account balance within 28 years, and annual payments of $3,360.00, keeping her account balance after 28 years, is $580.00. Our individual could receive $3,360.00+½($580.00)=$3,650.00 annually. The ½ factor extends the individual's account balance beyond 34 years instead of depleting the account balance within 28 years. Once the account balance is depleted (i.e. zero), the annual payments of $3,650.00 will come from the GENERAL account if the individual is still living. If the annual payments of $3,650.00 is below the expected living standards set by the government, then our single woman should apply to the welfare department for additional money.

Example 3: category 1(under 30 years of age)

In category 1, individuals are expected to work and contribute to their social security and medicare accounts during their 30 to 40 years of potential employment. If their average annual income is $20,000.00, then at 6% per year return rate, their social security and medicare account will be at least $268,000.00 after 30 years.

However, for example 3, let us assume that the individual is a single man who did not contribute that much to his social security and medicare account during his 30 or 40 years of potential employment. Let us assume that his account balance in the Social Security and Medicare Bank is only $250,000.00 instead of $268,000.00. If this individual retired at age 62, then his life expectancy, n, after retirement will be n=86-62=24 years. If we assume 6% return on investing his account balance and that his account balance will be depleted (i.e. zero) within 24 years, then according to the formula of chapter 6, the annual payments to the individual will be about $18,792.00. On the other hand, if we assume 6% return on investing his account balance keeping his account balance of $250,000.00 after 24 years, then the annual payments to the individual will be about $15,000.00. The difference between annual payments of $18,792.00, depleting his account balance within 24 years, and annual payments of $15,000.00, keeping his account balance after 24 years, is $3,792.00. Our individual could receive $15,000.00+½($3,792.00)=$16,896.00 annually. The ½ factor extends the individual account balance beyond 30 years instead of depleting the account balance within 24 years. Once the account balance is depleted (i.e. zero), the annual payments of $16,896.00 will come from the GENERAL account if the individual is still living. If the yearly distribution of $16,896.00 is below the expected living standards set by the government, then our single man should apply to the welfare department for additional money.

Example 4: category 1(under 30 years of age)

In category 1, individuals are expected to work and contribute to their social security and medicare accounts during their 30 to 40 years of potential employment. If their average annual income is $20,000.00, then at 6% per year return rate, their social security and medicare account will be at least $268,000.00 after 30 years.

However, for example 4, let us assume that the individual is a single woman who did not contribute that much to her social security and medicare account during her 30 or 40 years of potential employment. Let us assume that her account balance in the Social Security and Medicare Bank is only $250,000.00 instead of $268,000.00. If this individual retired at age 62, then her life expectancy, n, after retirement will be n=90-62=28 years. If we assume 6% return on investing her account balance and that her account balance will be depleted (i.e. zero) within 28 years, then according to the formula of chapter 6, the annual payments to the individual will be about $17,592.00. On the other hand, if we assume 6% return on investing her account balance keeping her account balance of $250,000.00 after 28 years, then the annual payments to the individual will be about $15,000.00. The difference between annual payments of $17592.00, depleting her account balance within 28 years, and annual payments of $15,000.00, keeping her account balance after 28 years, is $2592.00. Our individual could receive $15,000.00+½($2,592.00)=$16,296.00 annually. The ½ factor extends the individual's account balance beyond 34 years instead of depleting the account balance within 28 years. Once the account balance is depleted (i.e. zero), the annual payments of $16,296.00 will come from the GENERAL account if the individual is still living. If the yearly distribution of $16,296.00 is below the expected living standards set by the government, then our single woman should apply to the welfare department for additional money.

Example 5: category 2(30 years of age and older)

In category 2, many individuals do not have enough years during the 30 year transition period to build up their social security and medicare accounts.

For example 5, let us assume that the individual is a single man who did not contribute that much to his social security and medicare accounts during the 30 years of transition period. Let us assume that his account balance in the Social Security and Medicare Bank is only $56,000.00 instead of $268,000.00. If this individual retired at age 62, then his life expectancy, n, after retirement will be n=86-62=24 years. If we assume 6% return on investing his account balance and that his account balance will be depleted (i.e. zero) within 24 years, then according to the formula of chapter 6, the annual payments to the individual will be about $4,210.00. On the other hand, if we assume 6% return on investing his account balance keeping his account balance of $56,000.00 after 24 years, then the annual payments to the individual will be about $3,360.00. The difference between annual payments of $4,210.00, depleting his account balance within 24 years, and annual payments of $3,360.00, keeping his account balance after 24 years, is $850.00. Our individual could receive $3,360.00+½($850.00)=$3,785.00

annually. The ½ factor extends the individual account balance beyond 30 years instead of depleting the account balance within 24 years. Once the account balance is depleted (i.e. zero), the annual payments of $3,785.00 will come from the GENERAL account if the individual is still living. If the amount of $3,785.00 is less than the amount he would have received under the existing social security system then the balance in his Social Security and Medicare Bank accounts will be transferred to the GENERAL account, and our single man will then receive a yearly income to which he is entitled under the current social security system for the rest of his life.

Example 6: category 2(30 years of age and older)

In category 2, many individuals do not have enough years during the 30 year transition period to build up their social security and medicare accounts.

For example 6, let us assume that the individual is a single woman who did not contribute that much to her social security and medicare accounts during the 30 years of transition. Let us assume that her accounts balance in the Social Security and Medicare Bank is only $56,000.00 instead of $268,000.00. If this individual retired at age 62, then her life expectancy, n, after retirement will be n=90-62=28 years. If we assume 6% return on investing her account balance and that her account balance will be depleted (i.e. zero) within 28 years, then according to the formula of chapter 6, the annual payments to the individual will be about $3,940.00. On the other hand, if we assume 6% return on investing her account balance keeping her account balance of $56,000.00 after 28 years, then the annual payments to the individual will be about $3,360.00. The difference between annual payments of $3,940.00, depleting her account balance within 28 years, and annual payments of $3,360.00, keeping her account balance after 28 years, is $580.00. Our individual could receive $3,360.00+½($580.00)=$3,650.00 annually. The ½ factor extends the individual's account balance beyond 34 years instead of depleting the account balance within 28 years. Once the account balance is depleted (i.e. zero), the annual payments of $3,650.00 will come from the GENERAL account if the individual is still living. If the amount of $3,650.00 is less than the amount she would have received under the existing social security system then the balance in her Social Security and Medicare Bank accounts will be transferred to the GENERAL account, and our single woman will then receive the yearly income to which she is entitled under the current social security system for the rest of her life.

Example 7: category 2(30 years of age and older)

In category 2, many individuals do not have enough years during the 30 year transition period to build up their social security and medicare accounts.

For example 7, let us assume that the individual is a single man who did not contribute that much to his social security and medicare accounts during the 30 years of transition period. Let us assume that his account balance in the Social Security and Medicare Bank is $250,000.00 instead of $268,000.00. If this individual retired at age 62, then his life expectancy, n, after retirement will be n=86-62=24 years. If we assume 6% return on investing his account balance and that his account balance will be depleted (i.e. zero) within 24 years, then according to the formula of chapter 6, the annual payments to the individual will be about $18,792.00. On the other hand, if we assume 6% return on investing his account balance keeping his account balance of $250,000.00 after 24 years, then the annual payments to the individual will be about $15,000.00. The difference between annual payments of $18,792.00, depleting his account balance within 24 years, and annual payments of $15,000.00, keeping his account balance after 24 years, is $3,792.00. Our individual could receive $15,000.00+½($3792.00)=$16,896.00 annually. The ½ factor extends the individual's account balance beyond 30 years instead of depleting the account balance within 24 years. Once the account balance is depleted (i.e. zero), the annual payments of $16,896.00 will come from the GENERAL account if the individual is still living.If the amount of $16,896.00 is less than the amount he would have received under the existing social security system then the balance in his Social Security and Medicare bank account will be transferred to the GENERAL account, and our single man will then receive the yearly income to which he is entitled under the current social security system for the rest of his life.

Example 8: category 2(30 years of age and older)

In category 2, many individuals do not have enough years during the 30 year transition period to build up their social security and medicare accounts.

For example 8, let us assume that the individual is a single woman who did not contribute that much to her social security and medicare accounts during the 30 years of transition period. Let us assume that her account balance in the Social Security and Medicare Bank is $250,000.00 instead of $268000.00. If this individual retired at age 62, then her life expectancy, n, after retirement will be n=90-62=28 years. If we assume 6% return on investing her account balance and that her account balance will be depleted (i.e. zero) within 28 years, then according to the formula of chapter 6, the annual payments to the individual will be about $17,592.00. On the other hand, if we assume 6% return on investing her account balance keeping her account balance of $250,000.00 after 28 years, then the annual payments to the individual will be about $15,000.00. The difference between annual payments of $17592.00, depleting her account balance within 28 years, and annual payments of $15,000.00, keeping her account balance after 28 years, is $2,592.00. Our individual could receive $15,000.00+½($2,592.00)=$16,296.00 annually. The ½ factor extends the individual's account balance beyond 34 years instead of depleting the account balance within 28 years. Once the account balance is depleted (i.e. zero), the annual payments of $16,296.00 will come from the GENERAL account if the individual is still living. If the amount of $16,296.00 is less than the amount she would have received under the existing social security system then the balance in her Social Security and Medicare bank account will be transferred to the GENERAL account, and our single woman will then receive the yearly income to which she is entitled under the current social security system for the rest of her life.

Chapter 8

Social Security Payments to Married Individuals

A married couple that, either spouse or both, satisfied the 40 quarters requirement have their own social security accounts in the banks of the proposed social security system. The husband has his own account and the wife has her own account. At retirement, age 62 or older, the husband will receive an annual income from his account based on the formula derived in chapter 6. Similarly, at retirement, age 62 or older, the wife will receive an annual income from her account based on the formula derived in chapter 6. The life expectancy number of years after retirement, n, in the formula will be dictated by the national average of life expectancy plus 10 years. For example, if life expectancy for men is 76 and for women it is 80, then n in the formula will be n=(86–retirement age) years for men and n=(90–retirement age) years for women.

Example 1: Category 1(under 30 years of age)

Assume a married couple where the husband has $268,000.00 in his account and the wife has $200,000.00 in her account. If both, the husband and wife retired at age 62, then n=86-62=24 years is the life expectancy for the husband and n=90-62=28 years is the life expectancy for the wife.

Husband's payments:

If we assume 6% annual return on investing his account balance of $268,000.00 and that his account balance will be depleted (i.e. zero) within 24 years, then according to the formula of chapter 6, the annual payments to the husband will be about $20,145.00. On the other hand, if we assume 6% annual return on investing his account balance keeping his account balance of $268,000.00 after 24 years, then the annual payments to the husband will be about $16,080.00. The difference between annual payments of $20,145.00, depleting his account balance within 24 years, and annual payments of $16,080.00, keeping his account balance after 24 years, is $4,065.00. The husband could receive $16,080.00+½($4,065.00)=$18,112.50 annually. The ½ factor extends the husband's account balance beyond 30 years instead of depleting the account balance within 24 years. Once the account balance is depleted (i.e. zero), the annual payments of $18,112.50 will come from the GENERAL account if the husband is still living.

Wife's payments:

If we assume 6% annual return on investing her account balance of $200,000.00 and that her account balance will be depleted (i.e. zero) within 28 years, then according to the formula of chapter 6, the annual payments to the wife will be about $14,082.00. On the other hand, if we assume 6% annual return on investing her account balance keeping her account balance of $200,000.00 after 28 years, then the annual payments to the wife will be about $12,000.00. The difference between annual payments of $14,072.00, depleting her account balance within 28 years, and annual payments of $12,000.00, keeping her account balance after 28 years, is $2,072.00. The wife could receive $12,000.00+½($2,072.00)=$13,036.00 annually. The ½ factor extends the wife's account balance beyond 34 years instead of depleting the account balance within 28 years. Once the account balance is depleted (i.e. zero), the annual payments of $13,036.00 will come from the GENERAL account if the wife is still living.

Husband passes away:

Now assume that a few years after the husband's retirement, he passed away. The husband's account will be added to the wife's account and the balance of her account will be $468,000.00. The husband's account will be closed. The annual payments the wife receives will be based on her new account balance of $468,000.00 and her computed life expectancy of 28 years. Following the computation used above, the wife will receive an annual payment of $28,080.00   +1/2($32,930.00-$28,080.00)=$30,505.00.

When the wife passes away, her account will be closed and the balance of her account will be added to the GENERAL account in the Social Security and Medicare Bank.

Wife passes away:

Now assume that a few years after the wife's retirement, instead of the husband, the wife passes away. The wife's account will be added to the husband's account and the balance of his account will be $468,000.00. The wife's account will be closed. The annual payments the husband receives will be based on his new account balance of $468,000.00 and his computed life expectancy of 24 years. Following the computation used above, the husband will receive an annual payment of $28,080.00 +1/2($35178.00-$28,080.00)=$31,629.00. When the husband passes away, his account will be closed and the balance of his account will be added to the GENERAL account in the Social Security and Medicare Bank.

Combined husband and wife payments:

At the time of retirement, if the annual payment of $18,112.50+$13,036.00=$31,148.50 to the husband and wife is below the expected living standards set by the government, then our married couple should apply to the welfare department for public assistance.

Example 2: Category 1 (under 30 years of age)

Assume that the husband has $268,000.00 in his account and the wife has $20,000.00 in her account. If both, the husband and wife retired at age 62, then n=86-

62=24 years life expectancy for the husband and n=90-62=28 years life expectancy for the wife.

Husband's payments:

If we assume 6% annual return on investing his account balance of $268000.00 and that his account balance will be depleted (i.e. zero) within 24 years, then according to the formula of chapter 6, the annual payments to the husband will be about $20,145.00. On the other hand, if we assume 6% annual return on investing his account balance keeping his account balance of $268000.00 after 24 years, then the annual payments to the husband will be about $16,080.00. The difference between annual payments of $20,145.00, depleting his account balance within 24 years, and annual payments of $16,080.00, keeping his account balance after 24 years, is $4,089.00. The husband could receive $16,080.00+½($4,065.00)=$18,112.50 annually. The ½ factor extends the husband's account balance beyond 30 years instead of depleting the account balance within 24 years. Once the account balance is depleted (i.e. zero), the annual payments of $18,112.50 will come from the GENERAL account if the husband is still living.

Wife's payments:

If we assume 6% annual return on investing her account balance of $20,000.00 and that her account balance will be depleted (i.e. zero) within 28 years, then according to the formula of chapter 6, the annual payments to the wife will be about $1,408.00. On the other hand, if we assume 6% annual return on investing her account balance keeping her account balance of $20,000.00 after 28 years, then the annual payments to the wife will be about $1,200.00. The difference between annual payments of $1,407.00, depleting her account balance within 28 years, and annual payments of $1200.00, keeping her account balance after 28 years, is $207.00. The wife could receive $1,200.00+½($207.00)=$1,303.50 annually. The ½ factor extends the wife's account balance beyond 34 years instead of depleting the account balance within 28 years. Once the account balance is depleted (i.e. zero), the annual payments of $1,303.50 will come from the GENERAL account if the wife is still living.

Husband passes away:

Now assume that a few years after the husband's retirement, he passed away. The husband's account will be added to the wife's account and the balance of her account will be $288,000.00. The husband's account will be closed. The annual payments the wife receives will be based on her new account balance of $288,000.00 and her computed life expectancy of 28 years. Following the computation used above, the wife will receive an annual payment of $17,280.00 +1/2($20,264.00-$17,280.00)= $18,772.00. When the wife passes away, her account will be closed and the balance of her account will be added to the GENERAL account in the Social Security and Medicare Bank.

Wife passes away:

Now assume that a few years after the wife's retirement, instead of the husband, the wife passes away. The wife's account will be added to the husband's account and the balance of his account will be $288,000.00. The wife's account will be closed. The annual payments the husband receives will be based on his new account balance of $288,000.00 and his computed life expectancy of 24 years. Following the computation used above, the husband will receive an annual payment of $17,280.00 +1/2($21,648.00-$17,280.00)=$19,464.00. When the husband passes away, his account will be closed and the balance of his account will be added to the GENERAL account in the Social Security and Medicare Bank.

Combined husband and wife payments:

At the time of retirement, if the annual payment of $18,112.50+$1,303.50=$19,416.00 to the husband and wife is below the expected living standards set by the government, then our married couple should apply to the welfare department for public assistance.

Example 3: Category 1 (under 30 years of age)

Assume that the husband has $268,000.00 in his account and the wife has $0.00 in her account. If both, the husband and wife retired at age 62, then n=86-62=24 years life expectancy for the husband and n=90-62=28 years life expectancy for the wife.

Husband's payments:

If we assume 6% annual return on investing his account balance of $268,000.00 and that his account balance will be depleted (i.e. zero) within 24 years, then according to the formula of chapter 6, the annual payments to the husband will be about $20,145.00. On the other hand, if we assume 6% annual return on investing his account balance keeping his account balance of $268,000.00 after 24 years, then the annual payments to the husband will be about $16,080.00. The difference between annual payments of $20,145.00, depleting his account balance within 24 years, and annual payments of $16,080.00, keeping his account balance after 24 years, is $4089.00. The husband could receive $16,080.00+½($4,065.00)=$18,112.50 annually. The ½ factor extends the husband's account balance beyond 30 years instead of depleting the account balance within 24 years. Once the account balance is depleted (i.e. zero), the annual payments of $18,112.50 will come from the GENERAL account if the husband is still living.

Wife's payments:

If we assume 6% annual return on investing her account balance of $0.00 and that her account balance will be depleted (i.e. zero) within 28 years, then according to the formula of chapter 6, the annual payments to the wife will be $0.00. On the other hand, if we assume 6% annual return on investing her account balance keeping her account balance of $0.00 after 28 years, then the annual payments to the wife will still be $0.00. The difference between annual payments of $0.00, depleting her account balance within 28 years, and annual payments of $0.00, keeping her account balance after 28 years, is $0.00. The wife could receive $0.00+½($0.00)=$0.00 annually. The ½ factor extends the wife's account balance beyond 34 years instead of depleting the account balance within 28 years. Once the account balance is depleted (i.e. zero), the annual payments of $0.00 will come from the GENERAL account if the wife is still living.

Husband passes away:

Now assume that a few years after the husband's retirement, he passed away. The husband's account will be added to the wife's account and the balance of her account will be $268,000.00. The husband's account will be closed. The annual payments the wife receives will be based on her new account balance of $268,000.00 and her computed life expectancy of 28 years. Following the computation used above, the wife will receive an annual payment of $16,080.00   +1/2($18,857.00-$16,080.00)=$17,468.50. When the wife passes away, her account will be closed and the balance of her account will be added to the GENERAL account in the Social Security and Medicare Bank.

Wife passes away:

Now assume that after few years of the wife's retirement, instead of the husband, the wife passes away. The wife's account will be added to the husband's account and the balance of his account will still be $268,000.00. The wife's account will be closed. The annual payments the husband receives will be based on his new account balance of $268,000.00 and his computed life expectancy of 24 years. Following the computation used above, the husband will receive an annual payment of $16080.00 +1/2($20,145.00-$16,080.00)=$18,112.50. When the husband passes away, his account will be closed and the balance of his account will be added to the GENERAL account in the Social Security and Medicare Bank.

Combined husband and wife payments:

At the time of retirement, if the annual payment of $18,112.50+$0.00=$18,112.50 to the husband and wife is below the expected living standards set by the government, then our married couple should apply to the welfare department for public assistance.

Example 4: Category 2(30 years of age and older)

Assume that the husband has $100,000.00 in his account and the wife has $120,000.00 in her account. If both, the husband and wife retired at age 62, then n=86-62=24 years life expectancy for the husband and n=90-62=28 years life expectancy for the wife.

Husband's payments:

If we assume 6% annual return on investing his account balance of $100,000.00 and that his account balance will be depleted (i.e. zero) within 24 years, then according to the formula of chapter 6, the annual payments to the husband will be about $7,516.00. On the other hand, if we assume 6% annual return on investing his account balance keeping his account balance of $100,000.00 after 24 years, then the annual payments to the husband will be about $6,000.00. The difference between annual payments of $7,516.00, depleting his account balance within 24 years, and annual payments of $6,000.00, keeping his account balance after 24 years, is $1,526.00. The husband could receive $6,000.00+½($1,516.00)=$6,758.00 annually. The ½ factor extends the husband's account balance beyond 30 years instead of depleting the account balance within 24 years. Once the account balance is depleted (i.e. zero), the annual payments of $6758.00 will come from the GENERAL account if the husband is still living.

Wife's payments:

If we assume 6% annual return on investing her account balance of $120,000.00 and that her account balance will be depleted (i.e. zero) within 28 years, then according to the formula of chapter 6, the annual payments to the wife will be about $8,443.00. On the other hand, if we assume 6% annual return on investing her account balance keeping her account balance of $120,000.00 after 28 years, then the annual payments to the wife will be about $7,200.00. The difference between annual payments of $8,443.00, depleting her account balance within 28 years, and annual payments of $7,200.00, keeping her account balance after 28 years, is $1,243.00. The wife could receive $7,200.00+½($1,243.00)=$7,821.50 annually. The ½ factor extends the wife's account balance beyond 34 years instead of depleting the account balance within 28 years. Once the account balance is depleted (i.e. zero), the annual payments of $7,821.50 will come from the GENERAL account if the wife is still living.

Husband passes away:

Now assume that a few years after the husband's retirement, he passed away. The husband's account will be added to the wife's account and the balance of her account will be $220,000.00. The husband's account will be closed. The annual payments the wife receives will be based on her new account balance of $220,000.00 and her computed life expectancy of 28 years. Following the computation used above, the wife will receive an annual payment of $13,200.00 +1/2($15,480.00-$13,200.00)=$14340.00. When the wife passes away, her account will be closed and the balance of her account will be added to the GENERAL account in the Social Security and Medicare Bank.

Wife passes away:

Now assume that a few years after the wife's retirement, instead of the husband, the wife passes away. The wife's account will be added to the husband's account and the balance of his account will be $220,000.00. The wife's account will be closed. The annual payments the husband receives will be based on his new account balance of $220000.00 and his computed life expectancy of 24 years. Following the computation used above, the husband will receive an annual payment of $13200.00 +1/2($16,536.00-$13200.00)=$14,868.00. When the husband passes away, his account will be closed and the balance of his account will be added to the GENERAL account in the Social Security and Medicare Bank.

Combined husband and wife payments:

At the time of retirement, if the annual payment of $6,758.00+$7,821.50=$14,579.50 to the husband and wife is larger than the amount the couple would have received under the existing social security system, then they will receive the above annual payment. On the other hand, if the amount $14,579.50 is smaller than the amount the couple would have received under the existing social security system, then their accounts will be closed. The accounts balance will be added to the GENERAL account in the Social Security and Medicare Bank and they will receive the annual payment they are entitled to under the existing social security system.

Example 5: Category 2 (30 years of age and older)

Assume that the husband has $20,000.00 in his account and the wife has $80,000.00 in her account. If both, the husband and wife retired at age 62, then n=86-62=24 years life expectancy for the husband and n=90-62=28 years life expectancy for the wife.

Husband's payments:

If we assume 6% annual return on investing his account balance of $20,000.00 and that his account balance will be depleted (i.e. zero) within 24 years, then according to the formula of chapter 6, the annual payments to the husband will be about $1,505.00. On the other hand, if we assume

6% annual return on investing his account balance keeping his account balance of $20,000.00 after 24 years, then the annual payments to the husband will be about $1200.00. The difference between annual payments of $1,503.00, depleting his account balance within 24 years, and annual payments of $1,200.00, keeping his account balance after 24 years, is $303.00. The husband could receive $1200.00+½($303.00)=$1351.50 annually. The ½ factor extends the husband's account balance beyond 30 years instead of depleting the account balance within 24 years. Once the account balance is depleted (i.e. zero), the annual payments of $1351.50 will come from the GENERAL account if the husband is still living.

Wife's payments:

If we assume 6% annual return on investing her account balance of $80,000.00 and that her account balance will be depleted (i.e. zero) within 28 years, then according to the formula of chapter 6, the annual payments to the wife will be about $5,633.00. On the other hand, if we assume 6% annual return on investing her account balance keeping her account balance of $80,000.00 after 28 years, then the annual payments to the wife will be about $4,800.00. The difference between annual payments of $5,628.00, depleting her account balance within 28 years, and annual payments of $4,800.00, keeping her account balance after 28 years, is $828.00. The wife could receive $4,800.00+½($828.00)=$5,214.00 annually. The ½ factor extends the wife's account balance beyond 34 years instead of depleting the account balance within 28 years. Once the account balance is depleted (i.e. zero), the annual payments of $5,214.00 will come from the GENERAL account if the wife is still living.

Husband passes away:

Now assume that a few years after the husband's retirement, he passed away. The husband's account will be added to the wife's account and the balance of her account will be $100,000.00. The husband's account will be closed. The annual payments the wife receives will be based on her new account balance of $100,000.00 and her computed life expectancy of 28 years. Following the computation used above, the wife will receive an annual payment of $6,000.00 +1/2($7,036.00-$6,000.00)=$6,518.00. When the wife passes away, her account will be closed and the balance of her account will be added to the GENERAL account in the Social Security and Medicare Bank.

Wife passes away:

Now assume that a few years after the wife's retirement, instead of the husband, the wife passes away. The wife's account will be added to the husband's account and the balance of his account will be $100,000.00. The wife's account will be closed. The annual payments the husband receives will be based on his new account balance of $100,000.00 and his computed life expectancy of 24 years. Following the computation used above, the husband will receive an annual payment of $6,000.00 +1/2($7516.00-$6,000.00)=$6,758.00. When the husband passes away, his account will be closed and the balance of his account will be added to the GENERAL account in the Social Security and Medicare Bank.

Combined husband and wife payments:

At the time of retirement, if the annual payment of $1,351.50+$5,214.00=$6,565.50 to the husband and wife is larger than the amount the couple would have received under the existing social security system, then they will receive the above annual payment. On the other hand, if the amount $6,565.50 is smaller than the amount the couple would have received under the existing social security system, then their accounts will be closed. The accounts balance will be added to the GENERAL account in the Social Security and Medicare Bank and they will receive the annual payment they are entitled to under the existing social security system.

Example 6: Category 2(30 years of age and older)

Assume that the husband has $268,000.00 in his account and the wife has $0.00 in her account. If both, the husband and wife retired at age 62, then n=86-62=24 years life expectancy for the husband and n=90-62=28 years life expectancy for the wife.

Husband's payments:

If we assume 6% annual return on investing his account balance of $268,000.00 and that his account balance will be depleted (i.e. zero) within 24 years, then according to the formula of chapter 6, the annual payments to the husband will be about $20,145.00. On the other hand, if we assume 6% annual return on investing his account balance keeping his account balance of $268,000.00 after 24 years, then the annual payments to the husband will be about $16,080.00. The difference between annual payments of $20,145.00, depleting his account balance within 24 years, and annual payments of $16,080.00, keeping his account balance after 24 years, is $4,065.00. The husband could receive $16,080.00+½($4,065.00)=$18,112.50 annually. The ½ factor extends the husband's account balance beyond 30 years instead of depleting the account balance within 24 years. Once the account balance is depleted (i.e. zero), the annual payments of $18,112.50 will come from the GENERAL account if the husband is still living.

Wife's payments:

If we assume 6% annual return on investing her account balance of $0.00 and that her account balance will be depleted (i.e. zero) within 28 years, then according to the formula of chapter 6, the annual payments to the wife will be $0.00. On the other hand, if we assume 6% annual return on investing her account balance keeping her account balance of $0.00 after 28 years, then the annual payments to the wife will still be $0.00. The difference between annual payments of $0.00, depleting her account balance within 28 years, and annual payments of $0.00, keeping her account balance after 28 years, is $0.00. The wife could receive $0.00+½($0.00)=$0.00 annually. The ½ factor extends the wife's account balance beyond 34 years instead of depleting the account balance within 28 years. Once the account balance is depleted (i.e. zero), the annual payments of $0.00 will come from the GENERAL account if the wife is still living.

Husband passes away:

Now assume that a few years after the husband's retirement, he passed away. The husband's account will be added to the wife's account and the balance of her account will be $268,000.00. The husband's account will be closed. The annual payments the wife receives will be based on her new account balance of $268,000.00 and her computed life expectancy of 28 years. Following the computation used above, the wife will receive an annual payment of $16,080.00+1/2($18,857.00-$16,080.00)= $17,468.50. When the wife passes away, her account will be closed and the balance of her account will be added to the GENERAL account in the Social Security and Medicare Bank.

Wife passes away:

Now assume that a few years after the wife's retirement, instead of the husband, the wife passes away. The wife's account will be added to the husband's account and the balance of his account will be $268,000.00. The wife's account will be closed. The annual payments the husband receives will be based on his new account balance of $268,000.00 and his computed life expectancy of 24 years. Following the computation used above, the husband will receive an annual payment of $16,080.00 +1/2($20,145.00-$16,080.00)=$18,112.50. When the husband passes away, his account will be closed and the balance of his account will be added to the GENERAL account in the Social Security and Medicare Bank.

Combined husband and wife payments:

At the time of retirement, if the annual payment of $18,112.50+$0.00=$18,112.50 to the husband and wife is larger than the amount the couple would have received under the existing social security system, then they will receive the above annual payment. On the other hand, if the amount $18,112.50 is smaller than the amount the couple would have received under the existing social security system, then their accounts will be closed. The accounts balance will be added to the GENERAL account in the Social Security and Medicare Bank and they will receive the annual payment they are entitled to under the existing social security system.

Chapter 9

Social Security Payments to Divorced Individuals

In general, for all married couples, the date and the starting balance of their social security accounts and the date and account balances at the time of their divorce should be recorded. This information is needed to compute the amounts that will be used to settle the social security accounts between husband and wife. It is important to settle the accounts immediately after the divorce so that at actual distribution time there is no conflict and all accounts are in order. The fact that many couples divorce and some of these couples marry and divorce several times makes it imperative to settle the accounts immediately after any divorce. Since during married life, everything that the husband and wife have shared is equally (at the 50% split level), the amounts that they earned in their social security accounts during their married years should also be shared equally (split at the 50% level) immediately after the divorce.

Assume that a working couple after 10 years of marriage decided to call it quits and get divorced. Assume at the time they were married the husband's social security account balance was $60,000.00 and the wife's account balance was $40,000.00. At the time of their divorce, their account balances were $110,000.00 for the husband and $75,000.00 for the wife. To settle their accounts, first find the total amount the couple accumulated during their married years. Take the difference between the starting balances and the ending balances for both husband and wife. For the husband $110,000.00-$60,000.00=$50,000.00, and for the wife $75,000.00-$40,000.00=$35,000.00 for a total of $85,000.00. Now divide the total by two (50% split) to arrive at $42500.00, the amount that husband and wife should add to their balances just before they got married. Therefore, the husband's new balance will be $102,500.00 ($60,000.00+$42,500.00) and the wife's new balance will be $82,500.00 ($40,000.00+$42,500.00).

The above type of settlement is applicable for category 1 and category 2. At the time of retirement, if the individuals are single, then their distribution will follow the previous discussion of distribution to single individuals. If the individuals are married, then their distribution will follow the previous discussion of distribution to married individuals.

Chapter 10

Social Security Payments to Widowed Individuals

Married couples that are working have their own social security accounts. If the husband passed away after so many years of marriage, then the balance of his account should be either added to the wife's account at the time of the husband's death or used to help raise their children who are under age 16. Similarly, if the wife passed away after so many years of marriage, then the balance of her account should be either added to the husband's account at the time of the wife's death or used to help raise their children who are under age 16.

After the death of one spouse, and the wife or the husband remarry and reach the age of retirement, then the distribution will follow distribution to married couples. If the wife or husband remarry and divorce before reaching the retirement age, then the divorce settlement should have been reached immediately after the divorce as discussed in chapter 9. Also, if the wife or husband stayed divorced until reaching retirement age, the distribution will follow distribution to single individuals.

Chapter 11

Social Security Payments to Children of Deceased Individuals

Social security accounts are used to guarantee a good life for retired individuals. However, when one of the individuals passes away and leaves behind children under the age 16, then the social security account of the deceased could be used to help raise the children. Under our proposed plan, if the individual was married at the time of death, then the widow or widower does have an option of receiving the distribution from his or her deceased partner's social security account in the form of one payment or adding it on to her or his own social security account. In the case where the partner opted for adding it on his or her account, he or she cannot get welfare to raise the children. First, the social security account of the deceased has to be depleted. If the individual was married at the time of death and has children from a previous marriage, then the social security account of the deceased will be used to help raise all the deceased's children under age 16 regardless where the children live.

Chapter 12

Social Security Payments to Disabled Individuals

If an individual becomes disabled then his or her social security account will be used to pay for their care. The amount of distribution depends on the amount in their social security account. The limit of benefits is the balance of their account amount in the Social Security and Medicare Bank. Once their account is depleted, the disabled individual may seek assistance from the social welfare system.

Chapter 13

Medicare

The current Medicare system is complicated and costs the retirees and the government too much money. Many companies are taking advantage of loopholes in the current system, overcharging for their services and supplies. The cost of keeping the current Medicare system is staggering. Our aim is to provide excellent doctor and hospital care for all retirees at an affordable rate.

Table 7 shows the monthly income derived from Medicare premiums for $50, $75 and $100 monthly payments. As can be seen from the figures in table 7, the monthly income is in the billions. No wonder why insurance companies are competing and lobbying to keep health insurance costs rising. The insurance companies are the benefactors and they own a big share of the health providers in the USA. It is the intent of this book to show that health care could be very good and coverage could be affordable to every individual in the USA regardless of their health history.

The proposed health plan is 90/10, $0.0 deductible for hospital and doctor coverage with a maximum life time limit of $2 million per individual insured.

Table 7. Monthly income derived from monthly Medicare Premiums.

Individuals	$50/month Premium	$75/month Premium	$100/month Premium
30 million	$1.50 billion	$2.250 billion	$3.00 billion
33 million	$1.65 billion	$2.475 billion	$3.30 billion
36 million	$1.80 billion	$2.700 billion	$3.60 billion
39 million	$1.95 billion	$2.925 billion	$3.90 billion
42 million	$2.10 billion	$3.150 billion	$4.20 billion
45 million	$2.25 billion	$3.375 billion	$4.50 billion
48 million	$2.40 billion	$3.600 billion	$4.80 billion

Chapter 14

Discussion and Conclusion

Our plan for social security and Medicare is more effective and surely more desirable than the current social security and Medicare system. Remember, the current social security and Medicare system has to change for the benefit of all residents of the USA, and the only way to change it is by placing the change on the ballot for all citizens of the United States to vote. Do not depend on the politicians and government officials to change social security. Most of them are well to do and do not depend on the social security system nor Medicare. However, 90% of the United States population depends on social security and Medicare and it is your responsibility to change it. Do not criticize others for taking no action in changing the current social security and Medicare system. Instead, blame yourself for not taking any action to effect the change.

Large corporations do not buy health insurance for their employees, they insure them by retaining the insurance companies to handle the paper work only. The health insurance companies should provide health coverage to any individual at an affordable rate. If they are not willing to do so, the retired individuals should establish a **not for profit insurance company** to provide the coverage needed. With limited liability, there is no risk involved, and the new insurance company will thrive and provide competition for the existing insurance companies.